# Baby Memory book

Hello World!

DATE OF
BIRTH
_____

_____

TIME
_____

EYE
COLOR
_____

WEIGHT
_____

HEIGHT
_____

HOSPITAL
_____

DOCTOR
_____

# All About Me

MY FULL NAME IS _____

WHO CHOSE IT _____

MY NICKNAMES ARE _____

_____

_____

PEOPLE SAY I LOOK LIKE _____

_____

_____

FEATURES I GOT FROM MOMMY _____

_____

_____

FEATURES I GOT FROM DADDY _____

_____

_____

# All About Daddy

NAME _____

DATE OF BIRTH _____

PLACE OF BIRTH _____

OCCUPATION _____

FAVORITE MEAL _____

FAVORITE DESSERT _____

FAVORITE THINGS TO DO _____

| FAVORITE ACTIVITIES & HOBBIES | FAVORITE SHOWS & FILMS |
|---|---|
|  |  |

# All About Mommy

NAME

DATE OF BIRTH

PLACE OF BIRTH

OCCUPATION

FAVORITE MEAL

FAVORITE DESSERT

FAVORITE THINGS TO DO

## FAVORITE ACTIVITIES & HOBBIES

## FAVORITE SHOWS & FILMS

# How My Parents Found Out

_____
_____
_____
_____
_____
_____
_____
_____
_____
_____
_____
_____
_____
_____
_____
_____
_____

# A Letter to You as we watch you grow

_____

_____

_____

_____

_____

_____

_____

_____

_____

_____

_____

_____

_____

_____

_____

# Our Pregnancy Pictures

# MOOD AND ENERGY

_____

_____

_____

# CRAVING AND AVERSIONS

_____

_____

_____

# WHAT WAS GREAT

_____

_____

_____

# WHAT WAS CHALLENGING

_____

_____

_____

# Scan Pictures

# The story of how I was born

_____

_____

_____

_____

_____

_____

_____

_____

_____

_____

_____

_____

# Bringing me Home

_____

_____

_____

_____

# My First Home

ADDRESS

_____

_____

_____

_____

# My Family Tree
## Dads Side

**GRANDPARENTS NAMES**

**BUT I CALL THEM**

**MY SIBLING'S NAMES**

**DADDY'S SIBLING'S NAMES**

# My Family Tree
## Moms Side

**GRANDPARENTS NAMES**

**BUT I CALL THEM**

**MOM SIBLINGS NAMES**

# Our Family
# Tree

GRANDPARENTS

GREAT GRANDPARENTS

GRANDPARENTS

PARENTS

ME

# Our Family Photos

# My Handprint

DATE:

# My Footprint

DATE:

# Milestones

# My First Night at Home

# My First Bath

# My First Meal

# My First Trip Outside

# My First Tooth

# My First Smile

# Today, I Rolled over for the first time

# Today I crawled for the
## first time

# My First time sitting up

# Today I stood up for the first time

# My First Holiday

# My First Haircut

# My First Word

# My First Laugh

# First Week

# First Week

DATE

WEIGHT

H EIGHT

CUTE\FUNNY THINGS

THAT I CAN DO

_____

_____

_____

_____

THIS WEEK, I LEARNT

_____

_____

_____

_____

_____

# Second Week

# Second Week

DATE

WEIGHT

H EIGHT

CUTE\FUNNY THINGS

THAT I CAN DO

_____

_____

_____

_____

THIS WEEK, I LEARNT

_____

_____

_____

_____

# Third Week

# Third Week

DATE

WEIGHT

H EIGHT

CUTE\FUNNY THINGS

THAT I CAN DO

THIS WEEK, I LEARNT

# Fourth Week

# Fourth Week

**DATE**

**WEIGHT**

**HEIGHT**

**CUTE\FUNNY THINGS**

**THAT I CAN DO**

_____

_____

_____

_____

**THIS WEEK, I LEARNT**

_____

_____

_____

_____

_____

# ONE MONTH OLD

# One Month Old

DATE

WEIGHT

H EIGHT

CUTE\FUNNY THINGS

THAT I CAN DO

_____

_____

_____

_____

THIS MONTH, I LEARNT

_____

_____

_____

_____

# TWO MONTHS OLD

# Two Months Old

**DATE**

**WEIGHT**

**H EIGHT**

**CUTE\FUNNY THINGS**

**THAT I CAN DO**

_____

_____

_____

_____

**THIS MONTH, I LEARNT**

_____

_____

_____

_____

_____

_____

# THREE MONTHS OLD

# Three Months Old

**DATE**

**WEIGHT**

**HEIGHT**

**CUTE\FUNNY THINGS**

**THAT I CAN DO**

_____

_____

_____

_____

**THIS MONTH, I LEARNT**

_____

_____

_____

_____

_____

# 4 MONTHS OLD

# 4 Months Old

**DATE**

**WEIGHT**

**H EIGHT**

**CUTE\FUNNY THINGS**

**THAT I CAN DO**

_____

_____

_____

_____

**THIS MONTH, I LEARNT**

_____

_____

_____

_____

_____

# 5 MONTHS OLD

# 5 Months Old

**DATE**

**WEIGHT**

**H EIGHT**

**CUTE\FUNNY THINGS**

**THAT I CAN DO**

_____

_____

_____

_____

**THIS MONTH, I LEARNT**

_____

_____

_____

_____

_____

# 6 MONTHS OLD

# 6 Months Old

**DATE**

**WEIGHT**

**H EIGHT**

**CUTE\FUNNY THINGS**

**THAT I CAN DO**

_____

_____

_____

_____

**THIS MONTH, I LEARNT**

_____

_____

_____

_____

_____

_____

# 7 MONTHS OLD

# 7 Months Old

**DATE**

**WEIGHT**

**H EIGHT**

**CUTE\FUNNY THINGS**

**THAT I CAN DO**

_____

_____

_____

_____

**THIS MONTH, I LEARNT**

_____

_____

_____

_____

_____

# 8 MONTHS OLD

# 8 Months Old

| DATE | WEIGHT | H EIGHT |
|------|--------|---------|
|      |        |         |

CUTE\FUNNY THINGS
THAT I CAN DO
_____
_____
_____
_____

THIS MONTH, I LEARNT
_____
_____
_____
_____
_____
_____

# 9 MONTHS OLD

# 9 Months Old

**DATE**

**WEIGHT**

**HEIGHT**

**CUTE\FUNNY THINGS**

**THAT I CAN DO**

_____

_____

_____

_____

**THIS MONTH, I LEARNT**

_____

_____

_____

_____

_____

# 10 MONTHS OLD

# 10 Months Old

**DATE**

**WEIGHT**

**H EIGHT**

CUTE\FUNNY THINGS

THAT I CAN DO

_____

_____

_____

_____

THIS MONTH, I LEARNT

_____

_____

_____

_____

_____

# 11 MONTHS OLD

# 11 Months Old

DATE

WEIGHT

H EIGHT

CUTE\FUNNY THINGS

THAT I CAN DO

_____

_____

_____

_____

THIS MONTH, I LEARNT

_____

_____

_____

_____

# 12 MONTHS OLD

# 12 Months Old

DATE

WEIGHT

H EIGHT

CUTE\FUNNY THINGS

THAT I CAN DO

_____

_____

THIS MONTH, I LEARNT

_____

_____

_____

_____

I am ONE Today!

# Birthday Wishes

# Teeth Growth Chart

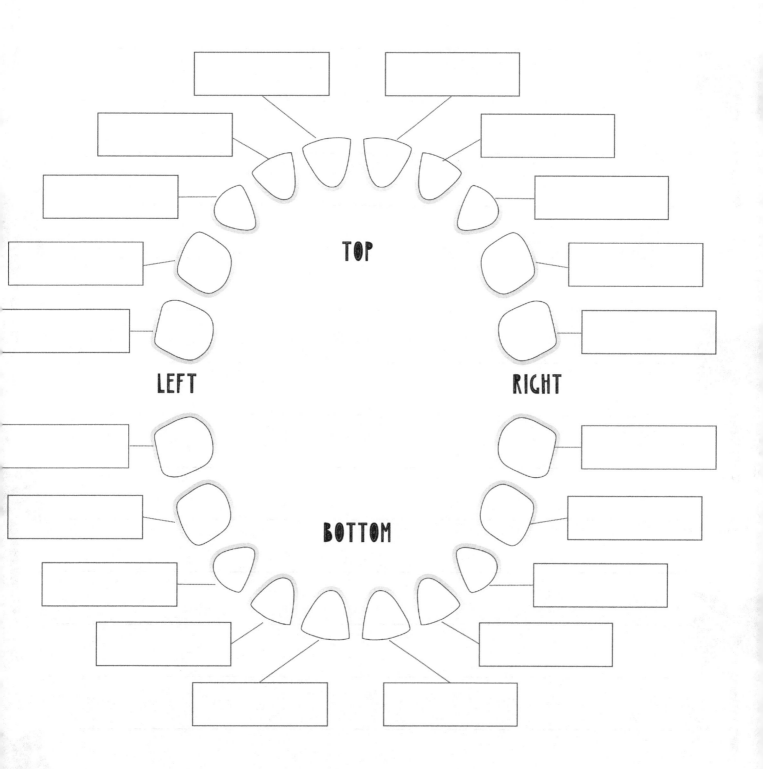

TOP

LEFT

RIGHT

BOTTOM

DATES THEY APPEARED

# Memories from my first year

# Memories from my first year

_____

_____

_____

_____

_____

_____

_____

_____

_____

_____

_____

_____

# Memories from my first year

# Memories from my first year

# Memories from my first year

# Memories from my first year

# Memories from my first year

_____

_____

_____

_____

_____

_____

_____

_____

_____

_____

_____

_____

# Memories from my first year

# Memories from my first year

# Memories from my first year

# Memories from my first year

# Memories from my first year

_____

_____

_____

_____

_____

_____

_____

_____

_____

_____

_____

_____

# Memories from my first year

# Memories from my first year

_____

_____

_____

_____

_____

_____

_____

_____

_____

_____

_____

_____

# Memories from my first year

# Memories from my first year

# Memories from my first year

# Memories from my first year

_____
_____
_____
_____
_____
_____
_____
_____
_____
_____
_____
_____
_____

# Memories from my first year

_____

_____

_____

_____

_____

_____

_____

_____

_____

_____

_____

_____

# Memories from my first year

# Memories from my first year

# Memories from my first year

# Memories from my first year

# Memories from my first year

# Memories from my first year

# Memories from my first year

_____

_____

_____

_____

_____

_____

_____

_____

_____

_____

_____

_____

# Memories from my first year

# Memories from my first year

# Memories from my first year

Made in the USA
Monee, IL
11 September 2024

65563078R00057